# A
# MAP BOOK
## for Bible Students

*By*

FREDERIC L. FAY

*Drawings by*

WILLIAM DUNCAN

SPIRE BOOKS

FLEMING H. REVELL COMPANY
OLD TAPPAN, NEW JERSEY

First printed in Great Britain 1967. An edition for the U.S.A. was published
by Whittemore Association, Inc., of Boston, Massachusetts.


ISBN 0-8007-8116-3

PALESTINE IN THE KNOWN WORLD OF JESUS' TIME

*Map 1*

Note tiny Palestine, with its capital city, Jerusalem, at the extreme eastern end of the Mediterranean Sea.

The little country of Palestine has had a greater influence on mankind than any other area of its size on earth. This is because it produced a literature preserved in what is called the Bible, a book which has been translated into over a thousand languages and dialects and is probably more widely read throughout the world than any other book. The influence of this book is not because of its literary merit, but principally because of its religious quality and message.

The great prophets of Old Testament time, as recorded in the Bible, were men of Palestine who made no claim to a message of their own devising. Rather, these men believed profoundly that God was using them as His voice to proclaim His message to His people. The writers at the beginning of the Christian era, also men of Palestine, told the world of the coming of Jesus the Son of God, and of his life, redemptive ministry and death. Thus Palestine was the cradle of Judaism and of Christianity.

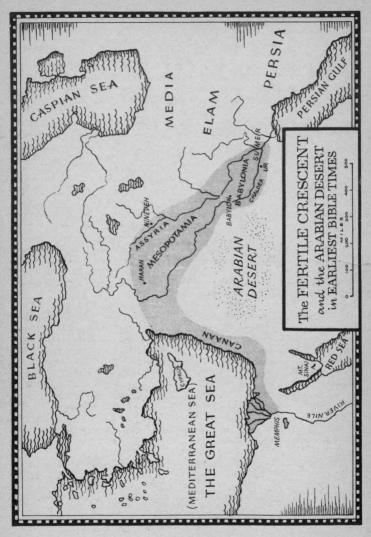

CASPIAN SEA

MEDIA

ELAM

PERSIA

PERSIAN GULF

BLACK SEA

NINEVEH

ASSYRIA

HARAN

MESOPOTAMIA

BABYLON

BABYLONIA

SUMER

CHALDEA

UR

ARABIAN DESERT

CANAAN

CYPRUS

MT. SINAI

RED SEA

(MEDITERRANEAN SEA)

THE GREAT SEA

MEMPHIS

RIVER NILE

The FERTILE CRESCENT
*and the* ARABIAN DESERT
in EARLIEST BIBLE TIMES

MILES
0   100   200   300   400   500

4

# THE FERTILE CRESCENT AND THE ARABIAN DESERT

*Map 2*

The earliest mentioned places in the Bible are in the region of the Tigris and Euphrates rivers at the head of the Persian Gulf. The area between these rivers, and for several miles outside each, is known as Mesopotamia. The word Mesopotamia means "between the rivers."

To the west and southwest is the Arabian desert. Fertile grazing country reached down along the shore of the Great Sea and extended to the mouth of the Nile River in Egypt. This curved area, reaching from the Persian Gulf on the east to the Nile delta on the west has been aptly termed the Fertile Crescent. In times of peace there was a constant stream of merchants passing back and forth over the main routes between Egypt and Mesopotamia, and in times of war armies passed over the same roads. It is believed that as early as 3500 B.C. there was a culture of high order in the extreme southern part, among the Sumerians, and later with the Assyrians and the Babylonians.

The land of Canaan on the shores of the Great Sea, which was to become the land of Israel, was about the size of the Principality of Wales, and was a bridge between the two great countries, east and west. Because of its location it was greatly influenced by these ancient civilizations in Mesopotamia and Egypt.

Especially was Israel affected by her contact with Mesopotamia. Out of that region came the arts of irrigation, cuneiform writing, architecture and sculpture, city and state organizations, magnificent textiles and finely carved gems. Abraham undoubtedly brought from Mesopotamia traditions and legends which were transmitted orally for centuries and then were recast by the fathers and teachers of Israel into graphic descriptions of the beginnings of things. Old forms became the channels of new pictures of truth. Among these were the stories of the creation of the world, of the beginning of mankind, the beginning of the knowledge of right and wrong, of strife, of racial and language variations.—all presented now with God as the center and Great Activator of life. Read Genesis, chapters 1-11.

It was in Mesopotamia that the Hebrews lived later, during their exile, and here they lived daily in the presence of a codified law, modes of worship, and the culture of that ancient civilization. They could not help being influenced by it. It was while in exile, and immediately after, that much of the Old Testament was written.

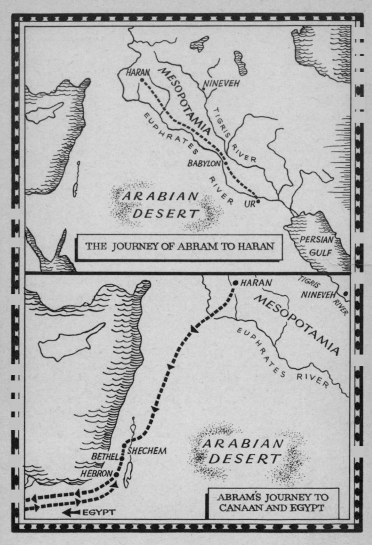

THE JOURNEY OF ABRAM TO HARAN

ABRAM'S JOURNEY TO CANAAN AND EGYPT

6

# THE JOURNEY OF ABRAM TO HARAN

*Map 3*                                                    *Genesis 11:31,32*

Abram was born and brought up in Ur of Chaldea, near the head of the Persian Gulf. Ur was a very ancient city, large, and dominated by a great temple devoted to the worship of the moon god. Many shrines devoted to other gods were conspicuous.

Abram's father, Terah, decided to move out of Ur. So, taking his family they went northwest following along the Euphrates River until they came to Haran at the top of the Fertile Crescent, and settled there. Haran was a flourishing city, a junction of the rich caravan trade between the cities of Mesopotamia, the Mediterranean shores, and Egypt. It was also a center of moon god worship. Here, after some years, Terah died.

## ABRAM'S JOURNEY TO CANAAN AND EGYPT

*Map 4*                                                 *Genesis 12 and 13.*

The Lord spoke to Abram at Haran and said—

*"Go from your country and your kindred and your father's house to the land that I will show you, and I will make of you a great nation, and I will bless you, and make your name great, so that you will be a blessing."*

So Abram went as the Lord told him, taking his family and his nephew Lot's family, and all their possessions and servants. They proceeded southwest into Canaan and passed through Shechem and Bethel, building an altar to the Lord in each place. They continued on to the dry, hilly country in the extreme south, known as the Negeb. A severe famine was in the land, so the nomadic group continued on down to Egypt. While living there, Abram became very rich in cattle and silver and gold; and Lot, also, acquired wealth in flocks and tents.

After some years Abram and his clan moved out of Egypt and journeyed back into the Negeb region, and to Bethel where he had first pitched his tent in Canaan.

For the rest of the story of Abram, read Genesis, chapters 14-25.

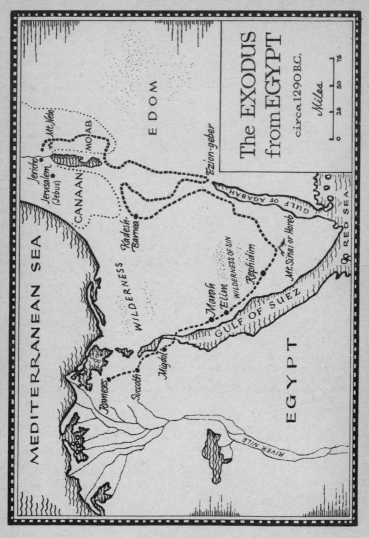

The EXODUS from EGYPT

circa 1290 B.C.

Miles
0   25   50   75

8

# THE EXODUS FROM EGYPT

The Pharaoh permitted the enslaved Hebrews to leave Egypt following a series of plagues that fell upon the Egyptians, even into the family of the Pharaoh. After the Hebrews moved out, the Pharaoh had a change of heart upon considering the loss of so many laborers, and the armies of Egypt were despatched to bring them back. The Hebrews became hemmed in by the Egyptians against the Red Sea near Migdol, but God sent a strong east wind which pushed back the waters and allowed them to cross to the other side. When the Egyptians followed, the waters came back and they were destroyed.

The Israelites continued southward and came to the rugged mountains near the tip of the Sinai penninsula. There Moses went up one of the mountains to meet with God and to renew covenant with Him. God called the Israelites to be His people and He gave them the Ten Commandments by the observance of which they would express their loyalty to Him. This acceptance of their covenant made them a self-conscious group.

At Sinai, also, God gave Moses directions for the building of a Tabernacle, a moveable tent with wooden walls to be a central sanctuary for worship, and to serve as a visible assurance to all the people, of the presence of the Lord with them on the journey.

The Israelites had been an unorganized rabble when they left Egypt, but they went away from Sinai with an awareness of their corporate identity, with a distinctive faith and purpose and a new way of living. They were no longer slaves but a people chosen by their God as His very own.

However, this latter fact did not save the Israelites from further troubles. As they moved north from Sinai, one crisis after another was met. But eventually they reached a point across the Jordan River just north of the Dead Sea, from which they could see into the land of Promise.

Moses was now old and knew that death was at hand. The old and honored leader of the children of Israel mounted the heights of Moab to stand on Mt. Nebo, and as he looked across into the land which had been promised to his forefathers, "The Lord said to him, 'This is the land of which I swore to Abraham, to Isaac, and to Jacob, I will give it to your descendants.' I have let you see it with your eyes, but you shall not go over there." So Moses the servant of the Lord died there in the land of Moab. (Deuteronomy 34:4,5).

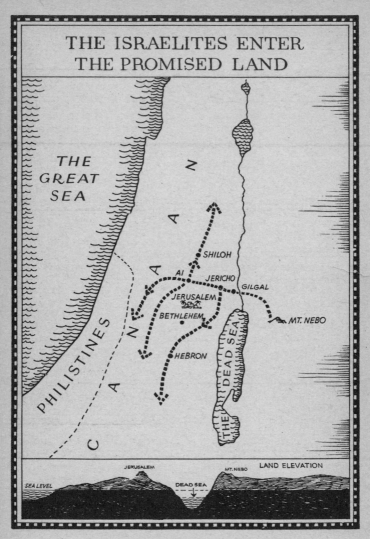

# THE ISRAELITES ENTER THE PROMISED LAND

THE GREAT SEA

C A N A A N

PHILISTINES

SHILOH

AI
JERICHO
GILGAL
JERUSALEM
BETHLEHEM
HEBRON

MT. NEBO

THE DEAD SEA

LAND ELEVATION

SEA LEVEL
JERUSALEM
DEAD SEA
MT. NEBO

# THE ISRAELITES ENTER THE PROMISED LAND

Shortly before Moses' death, he appointed Joshua to be his successor. Joshua had proved his ability during the stay in the wilderness, and was fully qualified to lead the Hebrew invasion into Canaan. When Joshua gave the word to advance and cross the Jordan, the priests bearing the Ark of the Covenant went first. According to the biblical account, when the feet of the priests bearing the Ark dipped in the water at the edge of the Jordan, the river divided, and all Israel walked over on the dry bed of the river. The priests who bore the Ark of the Covenant stood in the middle of the river bed until the last Israelite had passed over.

Then Joshua, at God's command, had a man from each of the twelve tribes take a stone from the spot on the river bed where the priests stood and carry them to the place where they lodged the first night across. As the reason for doing this, Joshua explained:

> "When your children ask their fathers in time to come, 'what do these stones mean?' then you shall let your children know, 'Israel passed over this Jordan on dry ground.' For the Lord your God dried up the waters of the Jordan for you until you passed over."

The priests went up from the bed of the river and the waters of the Jordan started rolling by as they had done before.

Thus at last the Children of Israel had arrived in the Promised Land which God had designated for their fathers five centuries before.

They now moved inland a short way and established a new camp, with the Tabernacle and altar in the center, and the tents of the various tribes around them. They called the place Gilgal.

From Gilgal they continued on and laid siege to a strong-walled city named Jericho. This city they captured and utterly destroyed.

Joshua now moved rapidly, attacking one place after another in quick succession—north, south, and westward, until soon the Israelites were settled in the central part of Canaan. Thus ended the first phase of the invasion and possession.

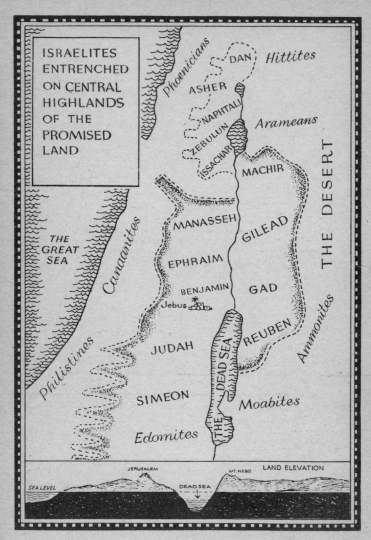

ISRAELITES
ENTRENCHED
ON CENTRAL
HIGHLANDS
OF THE
PROMISED
LAND

Phoenicians

Hittites

DAN

ASHER

NAPHTALI

Arameans

ZEBULUN

ISSACHAR

MACHIR

Canaanites

THE
GREAT
SEA

MANASSEH

GILEAD

THE DESERT

EPHRAIM

BENJAMIN

GAD

Jebus

Philistines

JUDAH

DEAD SEA

REUBEN

Ammonites

SIMEON

Moabites

THE

Edomites

LAND ELEVATION

JERUSALEM

MT. NEBO

SEA LEVEL

DEAD SEA

# ISRAELITES ENTRENCHED ON CENTRAL HIGHLANDS OF THE PROMISED LAND

*Map 7*

During the temporary rest from war, following the preliminary conquering of the Promised Land, Joshua portioned out the land to the various tribes of Israel according to the earlier plan of Moses. The Israelites were fairly well entrenched in the hill and mountain regions in the central highlands, but the Canaanites were more than a match for the invaders in the lowland areas.

The rich, fertile coastal plain still remained with the Philistines, Canaanites, and Phoenicians. Large valleys running east and west between mountain ranges, were still controlled by the natives, and even "the Jebusites, the inhabitants of Jerusalem, the people of Judah could not drive out; so the Jebusites dwelt with the people of Judah at Jerusalem to this day." (Joshua 15:63)

There was no unity or central authority among the Israelites. Each tribe was ruled by a judge who had won temporary leadership through military prowess in an emergency. Each tribe fought for itself against the natives in its immediate vicinity, and at times even against other Hebrew tribes. It was an era of great lawlessness and of turning away from the Hebrew God. Again and again in the book of Judges is repeated this sentence, "And the people of Israel again did what was evil in the sight of the Lord." In fact, the final summarizing verse for the entire history of this period (the book of Judges) is, "In those days there was no king in Israel; every man did what was right in his own eyes." (21:25)

The constant fear of attack from the native inhabitants anywhere along their borderline forced the tribes of Israelites to unite. They asked the prophet Samuel to appoint a king who should direct them. Under the guidance of God, Samuel chose a young man named Saul and he was enthusiastically accepted by the Israelites as their king. (I Samuel 10)

(For the account of Saul as king, read I Samuel, chapters 10 through 15).

As time went on, Saul deliberately failed to follow the voice of God in his reign and trouble came to him and his people. Samuel had to tell the king that as he, Saul, had rejected God, so God rejected him as king. In discouragement and despair, Saul took his own life. Thus passed the first king of the Israelites.

13

PALESTINE

ONE KINGDOM
UNDER DAVID
AND SOLOMON

C. 1000 – 925 B.C.

PHOENICIA

THE
GREAT
SEA

J U D A H

PHILISTINES

BETHEL
JERICHO
JERUSALEM
BETHLEHEM

HEBRON

SALT SEA

# PALESTINE—ONE KINGDOM
# UNDER DAVID AND SOLOMON

*Map 8*

The second king of the Israelites was David. One of his first acts as ruler was to capture the stronghold of the Jebusites, which he renamed Jerusalem, and made it the capital city for his people. To this place he brought the Ark of the Covenant as the symbol of the Presence of God in their midst. David's armies drove back and conquered many of the enemy on the border of Saul's kingdom, and extended its boundaries until he held sway from the Great Sea on the west to the desert beyond the Jordan on the east, and from the Red Sea in the south to the River Euphrates in the north.

In his later years, David had to combat revolts among his own people, as well as drought, famine, and a plague. Aged and weary, he felt his end approaching. Then he called to him his son Solomon and charged that he should walk in the ways of God, and keep His commandments and ordinances. The biblical account of David closes with these words—"and David slept with his fathers and was buried in the city of David." (I Kings 2:10).

(The reign of King David is recorded in II Samuel-I Kings 2:10)

The third king was Solomon. King Solomon was a great builder, and seemingly obsessed to become a powerful ruler whose splendor might rival that of Egypt and Babylonia. First, he constructed a series of fortresses to protect his frontiers. Then he turned his efforts to build a magnificent palace for himself and a temple to show his devotion to the God of Israel. He sought the help of Hiram, King of Tyre, in Phoenicia, to plan the buildings and provide the lumber.

Solomon had a large standing army which necessitated the building of living quarters and roads to move them. To do all this he had to resort to forced labor and even slavery to provide the hundreds of thousands of men necessary for the work. The cost of this construction was enormous. It put a tremendous burden on the people, so great that it brought them to near rebellion. When Solomon finally died, the great structure of the kingdom reared by his father David, and which he himself had tried to enlarge and strengthen, was broken beyond repair, and the Hebrew kingdom was in ruins.

(For Solomon's reign read I Kings 2:12—11:43)

THE TWO
KINGDOMS
OF JUDAH
AND ISRAEL
C. 850–721 B.C.

PHOENICIA

THE
GREAT
SEA

ISRAEL

SAMARIA

SHECHEM

PHILISTIA

BETHEL

JERICHO

JERUSALEM

BETHLEHEM

HEBRON

SALT SEA

JUDAH

Miles

0   10   20   30   40

# THE TWO KINGDOMS

*Map 9*                                    *I Kings 12—II Kings 17.*

Solomon's son. Rehoboam was crowned in Jerusalem as the new king. However, a rebellious spirit was burning among the masses, especially in the northern tribes who were suspicious of any king in the south, since Solomon had brought great hardship upon the people through his lavish extravagances and his insistence on forced labor.

So the northern tribes called in one of their number, Jeroboam, and had him crowned in Shechem as the king of their state which they called Israel, to offset Judah and their king Rehoboam. Naturally the relations between these two kingdoms were not very friendly. Occasionally they did join in action against a common enemy, but at other times they fought against each other.

Some years later the capital of the northern kingdom was transferred from Shechem to Samaria, high up on a hilltop overlooking a broad and flourishing plain in the center of their state. Here they built a stronghold which made a good defence for the protection of their capital, even as Jerusalem in the southern kingdom was located on the hill of the Jebusites and was impregnable to her foes.

*Rehoboam and the division of the kingdom—J.S. Von Carolsfeld*

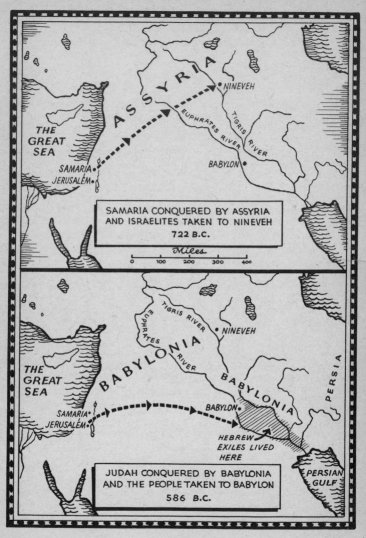

THE GREAT SEA

ASSYRIA

NINEVEH

EUPHRATES RIVER

TIGRIS RIVER

SAMARIA
JERUSALEM

BABYLON

SAMARIA CONQUERED BY ASSYRIA
AND ISRAELITES TAKEN TO NINEVEH
722 B.C.

Miles
0    100   200   300   400

TIGRIS RIVER

NINEVEH

EUPHRATES RIVER

THE GREAT SEA

BABYLONIA

BABYLONIA

PERSIA

SAMARIA
JERUSALEM

BABYLON

HEBREW
EXILES LIVED
HERE

PERSIAN
GULF

JUDAH CONQUERED BY BABYLONIA
AND THE PEOPLE TAKEN TO BABYLON
586 B.C.

# SAMARIA CONQUERED BY ASSYRIA AND ISRAELITES
## DEPORTED TO NINEVEH
### 722 B.C.

*Map 10*                                                          *II Kings 17*

Israel and Judah were unable to build a single front against their enemies since they were each too occupied with the concerns of their own territory. For two centuries Israel had a series of kings, most of whom ascended the throne after murdering their predecessors. Civil war kept the government constantly in a state of upheaval. Hostile neighboring peoples were always a threat. The Israelites forsook the Lord their God who had brought them up out of captivity in Egypt. In 722 B.C. the king of Assyria besieged Samaria the capital city of the northern kingdom, captured it, and carried away many of the Israelites to Assyria from whence they never returned.

# JUDAH CONQUERED BY BABYLONIA
## AND THE PEOPLE TAKEN TO BABYLON
### 586 B.C.

*Map 11*                                                   *II Kings 24 and 25.*

After a hundred years, the power of Assyria waned, while that of Babylon in the south, increased greatly. The kings of Babylon, one after the other, reached out and conquered Assyria, thus controlling all of Mesopotamia.

Nebuchadnezzar the king of Babylon wanted to be free to go along the shore of the Great Sea in order to have unhindered access to Egypt to the south. So his armies went over and seized Judah with its capital city of Jerusalem. They despoiled the Temple of its treasures, broke down the city wall, and carried away the royal family and thousands of the people of Jerusalem as prisoners of war to Babylon. Now Babylon controlled the whole of the Fertile Crescent from the Tigris and Euphrates to Egypt.

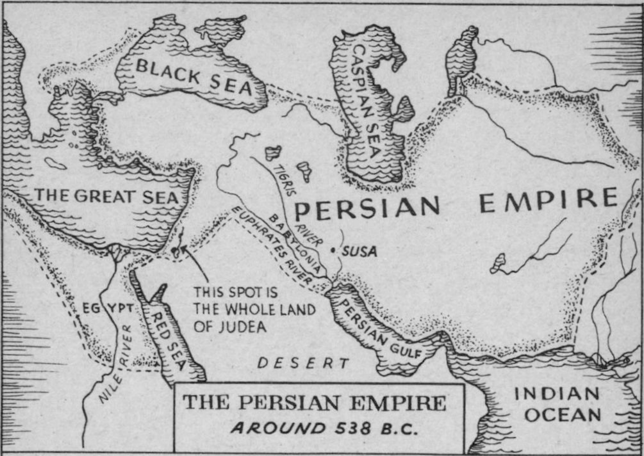

BLACK SEA

CASPIAN SEA

THE GREAT SEA

PERSIAN EMPIRE

TIGRIS RIVER

EUPHRATES RIVER

BABYLONIA

• SUSA

EGYPT

RED SEA

NILE RIVER

THIS SPOT IS
THE WHOLE LAND
OF JUDEA

PERSIAN GULF

DESERT

INDIAN
OCEAN

**THE PERSIAN EMPIRE**
*AROUND 538 B.C.*

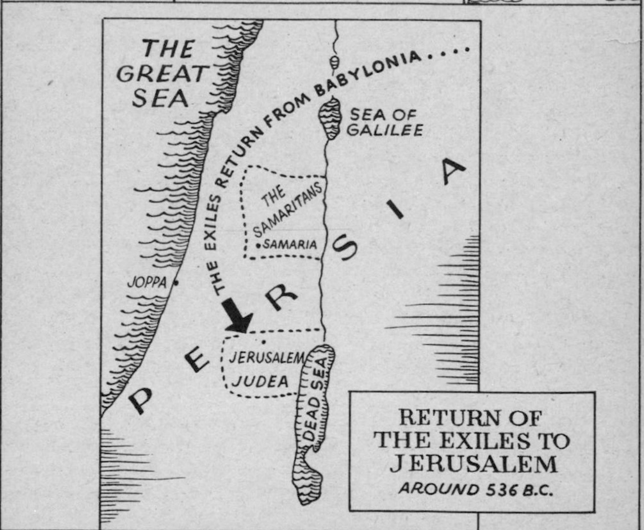

THE
GREAT
SEA

THE EXILES RETURN FROM BABYLONIA....

SEA OF
GALILEE

THE
SAMARITANS

• SAMARIA

JOPPA •

P E R S I A

JERUSALEM

JUDEA

DEAD SEA

**RETURN OF
THE EXILES TO
JERUSALEM**
*AROUND 536 B.C.*

# THE PERSIAN EMPIRE
## Around 538 B.C.

*Map 12*

About 50 years went by, during which the mighty power of Babylon weakened. But over in the east a new empire showed itself. Persia, under the kingship of Cyrus, was rapidly expanding and giving signs of becoming a power with which to reckon. The armies of Cyrus moved westward and soon had taken possession of all the land, and more, formerly ruled by Babylon. Over by the Great Sea, between its shore and the Dead Sea was the now tiny land of Judah, about 20 by 30 miles in size, an area comparable perhaps, with Greater London.

Among the exiles still in Babylon was a prophet whose name is unknown, but who is commonly referred to as the second Isaiah. He, somehow, believed that God had chosen Cyrus to be His instrument to set the Hebrew captives free and allow them to go back and rebuild Jerusalem. The message of this prophet to his people is found in Isaiah 44:24-28; 45:1-13. Also Isaiah, chapter 40.


# RETURN OF THE EXILES TO JERUSALEM
## Around 536 B.C.

*Map 13*                                     *The books of Ezra and Nehemiah.*

The prophet had been right. Read Ezra, chapter 1. However, when Cyrus granted permission for the Jewish exiles to return to Jerusalem, only a small number responded. Many of the Jews had married and established homes in exile. The land of their fathers was but a faint memory to them. Many had been born in Babylonia. They were more interested in the present than the past.

Those who did go back to Judah took with them the vessels which Nebuchadnezzar had carried away from the Temple at Jerusalem. After the difficult journey back across the desert, the outlook in their homeland was forlorn and depressing. Jerusalem was a heap of ruins. The fields, choked with weeds and rubbish, had to be cleared before they could be tilled. If, back in Babylon, the exiles had had glorious dreams of rebuilding the house of the Lord and the Holy City, those dreams were rudely shattered by the conditions they faced on their return to Jerusalem. They were in constant struggle merely to keep themselves alive.

However, they did keep on. More exiles returned, and after nearly a century a new Temple had been erected, the walls of the city rebuilt, and the Jews had at least the semblance of a kingdom of their own once more. (445 B.C.) The events of this period are vividly recorded in the books of Ezra and Nehemiah.

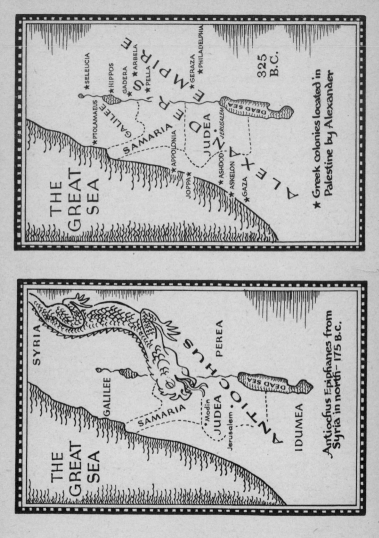

**Top map:**

SELEUCIA

HIPPOS

GADERA

ARBELA

PELLA

GERAZA

PHILADELPHIA

325 B.C.

PTOLAMAEUS

GALILEE

APPOLONIA

SAMARIA

JUDEA

JERUSALEM

JOPPA

ASHDOD

ASKELON

GAZA

DEAD SEA

SYRIA'S EMPIRE

ALEXANDER

THE GREAT SEA

★ Greek colonies located in Palestine by Alexander

**Bottom map:**

SYRIA

GALILEE

SAMARIA

JUDEA

Modin

Jerusalem

PEREA

IDUMEA

DEAD SEA

ANTIOCHUS

THE GREAT SEA

Antiochus Epiphanes from Syria in north- 175 B.C.

22

# GREEK COLONIES LOCATED IN PALESTINE
## by Alexander the Great

*Map 14*

About 333 B.C., Alexander the Great came down from the north and led his armies into the Persian Empire along the eastern coast of the Great Sea. Despite the ferocity and ruthlessness of Alexander, his great purpose apparently was to scatter through the world the seeds of Greek culture and civilization. Following this plan, he permitted the Jews great liberty in their religion and ways of living, but at the same time he established in all parts of Palestine peaceful Greek settlements or colonies.

The result was that the Jews were constantly in touch with Greek thought and ways and came to feel at home with them. The new Greek culture seemed to many of the Jews much more attractive than their own and they accepted and adopted much of it. Alexander's influence upon the Jews in Palestine was more significant than that of any non-Jew in history. Alexander died about 323 B.C. at the age of 33.


# ANTIOCHUS EPIPHANES
## (An-tī'-okus Ē-p̂if'-an-ēs)
## from Syria in the North—175 B.C.

*Map 15*

Upon the death of Alexander, his empire was divided. Syria to the north became a strong power, as did Egypt to the south. Palestine was the bridge between the two, and armies were constantly tramping back and forth as each great power alternately surged toward the other.

Antiochus Epiphanes became king of Syria in 175 B.C. and soon started a terror siege to wipe out Judaism. He ordered that no more should the Sabbath be observed, nor should the difference between ceremonially clean and unclean food be recognized. He set up heathen altars and erected shrines to Zeus in the Jewish Temple. As a crowning insult he offered in the Temple a sacrifice of swine to the Olympian Zeus. Immediate execution was the penalty for anyone possessing a copy of the Jewish Law. Many Jews preferred death rather than give up their religious traditions.

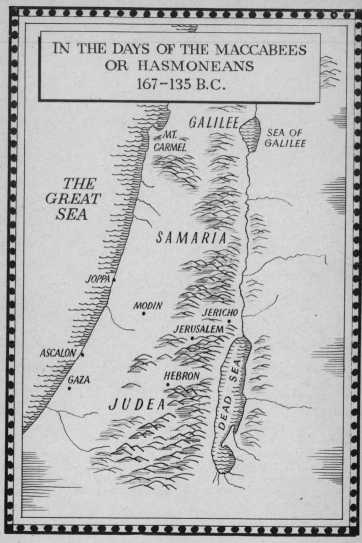

IN THE DAYS OF THE MACCABEES
OR HASMONEANS
167-135 B.C.

GALILEE

MT. CARMEL

SEA OF GALILEE

THE GREAT SEA

SAMARIA

JOPPA

MODIN

JERICHO

JERUSALEM

ASCALON

GAZA

HEBRON

DEAD SEA

JUDEA

# IN THE DAYS OF THE MACCABEES
(Sometimes called "Hasmoneans" because of Hashmon,
an ancestor of the Maccabees)
167 to 135 B.C.


*Map 16*


During the terrible years under Antiochus Epiphanes, there were many Jews who refused to give up their religious tradition and offer sacrifice on a heathen altar, as commanded. Among these was Mattathias, a man with five sons, living in the little town of Modin, situated on the hills of Judea, some 20 miles northwest of Jerusalem. When a Syrian officer was encouraging Jews to make the heathen sacrifice, Mattathias killed the soldier and destroyed the altar. Then he, his sons and other desperate zealots took to the mountains and set up guerilla warfare, a tiny band of untrained rebels against the disciplined hosts of Syrian soldiers. They overturned the hated altars and struck down the apostate Jews who sacrificed on them. They attacked the enemy in narrow mountain passes.


Finally Mattathias died and was succeeded by his son Judas who was given the name of Maccabeus, or the Hammerer. Under Judas, the Jews recovered and restored the Temple which had been desecrated by Antiochus. It was a day of great rejoicing, in 165 B.C. when the Temple was re-consecrated. An eight-day feast was held in honor of the occasion. Joyful meals were in order, houses were brightly lighted and religious services attended. Remembrance of this happy time is perpetuated in the Feast of Lights, and in the Jewish Hanukka observance today.


Judas was eventually killed in action, but was immediately replaced by his brother Jonathan. Then Jonathan was taken prisoner and put to death, to be in turn succeeded by his brother Simon. By the time Simon died in 135 B.C., thirty years after the recovery of the Temple, the province over which Antiochus Epiphanes had so frightfully trampled was now being left alone, and was enjoying considerable independence.

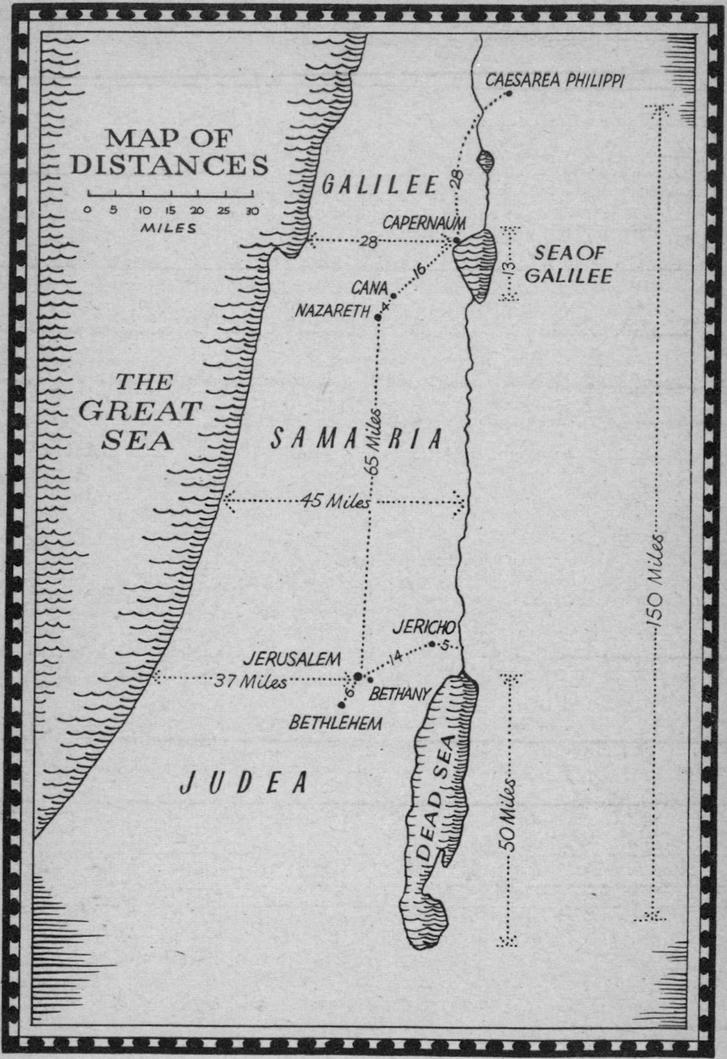

MAP OF DISTANCES

0 5 10 15 20 25 30
MILES

CAESAREA PHILIPPI

GALILEE

28

CAPERNAUM

28

SEA OF
GALILEE

16

13

CANA

NAZARETH

4

THE
GREAT
SEA

SAMARIA

65 Miles

45 Miles

150 Miles

JERICHO

5

JERUSALEM

14

37 Miles

6

BETHANY

BETHLEHEM

JUDEA

DEAD SEA

50 Miles

# MAP OF DISTANCES

*Map 17*

Palestine is a strip of country approximately 150 miles long, north and south, and 50 or 60 miles wide.

The common method of travel in Palestine in Jesus' day was on foot. People traveled only when obliged to as it was a slow, tiresome, and often dangerous business. If rarely one rode, it was on the back of a donkey.

Travel on foot would average perhaps sixteen miles a day. The distance from Nazareth to Jerusalem by the customary route along the east side of the Jordan was about seventy miles, and such a walking trip must have taken five days. It is quite evident that Jesus, either alone or with his disciples, made this journey many times. In addition, he was constantly going from place to place in Galilee and surrounding countries in his ministry with the people.

The flight into Egypt when Jesus was a baby must have covered at least 200 miles each way, though probably there was a donkey for Mary and the baby, while Joseph walked by their side.

The roads in Palestine were hardly more than paths, except where the Romans had built good main highways for commercial and military purposes.

## HEBREW LINEAR MEASURE
### Named from members of the human body

*Finger breadth (Jeremiah 52:21)*—a little more than 3/4 inch.

*Hand breadth (I Kings 7:26)*—width of a man's four fingers laid flat, just over 3½ inches.

*Span (I Samuel 17:4)*—the measure from the thumb to the little finger expanded, about 9 inches.

*Cubit (Deuteronomy 3:11)*—the measure of a man's arm from elbow to the end of the middle finger, about 18 inches.

*Fathom (Acts 27:28)*—The full stretch of the two arms from tip to tip of the middle finger, 5 or 6 feet.

*Reed (Ezekiel 40:5)*—Six cubits, 9 feet.

*Furlong (Matthew 14:24)*—Four hundred cubits, 600 feet.

*Roman Mile (Matthew 5:41)*-About 1860 feet, less than an English mile.

*Sabbath Day's Journey (Acts 1:12)*—Usually considered as 200 cubits, or 3000 feet, which was the distance by which the Ark preceded the Israelites on the journey to the Promised Land. Since they were allowed to worship at the Ark, this minimum distance was permitted on the Sabbath. The Mount of Olives was a Sabbath day's journey across the Valley of the Kidron from Jerusalem.

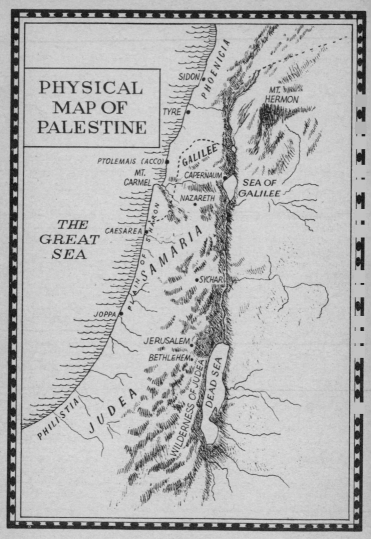

PHYSICAL
MAP OF
PALESTINE

SIDON

PHOENICIA

TYRE

MT.
HERMON

PTOLEMAIS (ACCO)

GALILEE

MT.
CARMEL

CAPERNAUM

SEA OF
GALILEE

NAZARETH

THE
GREAT
SEA

CAESAREA

PLAINS OF SHARON

SAMARIA

SYCHAR

JOPPA

JERUSALEM

BETHLEHEM

DEAD SEA

PHILISTIA

JUDEA

WILDERNESS OF JUDEA

# PHYSICAL MAP OF PALESTINE

*Map 18*

The physical surface of Palestine varies greatly. A study of this map shows that moving from west to east there are four natural strips running north and south. First is the COASTAL PLAIN. This begins with the Philistine Plain at the south. It was here the Philistines landed in the 12th century B.C. and occupied this area. The name, Palestine, is a derivation from Philistine. Then comes the Plain of Sharon extending roughly from Joppa to Caesarea. From Mt. Carmel northward around the harbor to Acco (later called Ptolemais) is a strip of plain that extends beyond Phoenicia. This entire coastal strip of Palestine would probably average 15 miles in width.

The second physical section is the HIGHLAND RIDGE which is a sort of backbone for Palestine. Just southwest of the Sea of Galilee, the backbone is temporarily broken by a belt of lower hill country extending to and including the Plain of Esdraelon along the side of Mt. Carmel. Then the mountainous ridge begins to heighten again until in upper Galilee it attains to more than 3000 feet.

The third strip is the JORDAN VALLEY, which is a deep cut in the earth's surface at the bottom of which flows the Jordan River. The Jordan has its beginnings in the Lebanon mountains to the north, and flows south through tiny Merom Lake, sometimes called Huleh. Then it continues on through the Sea of Galilee, which is about 700 feet below sea level, and emerges once more as a river. It makes a winding course, and at times the valley becomes very narrow. Much of the land is well covered with trees, and wild animals abound. Read Jeremiah 12:5. Eventually it empties into the Dead Sea as its final destination, for this body of water has no outlet. This causes an extremely salty condition, so great that it can sustain no life. The water line of the Dead Sea is about 1300 feet below sea level, while the bottom is another 1300 feet below that.

The fourth strip is east of the Jordan,—the TRANS-JORDAN PLATEAU, which is nearly 4000 feet high, and crossed by several rivers which flow into the Jordan. This trans-Jordan area contains cities and regions mentioned in the Old Testament, as well as the New Testament country of Perea, and Decapolis with its ten major cities.

So we find that this tiny land of Palestine presents a great contrast in its physical surface. Snow-capped Mt. Hermon in the north rises to a height of 9000 feet,—over one and one-half miles, while the Dead Sea in the south is the lowest spot found anywhere on the earth's surface.

# HEBREW CHRONOLOGY

*Most of these dates must be considered approximate*

1020 B.C.  Saul anointed first king of Israelites.

1000 B.C.  David, king of Israelites.

962 B.C.  Solomon succeeds his father David as king. He carries out an extensive building program, including the Temple. palaces and roads.

935 B.C.  The Divided Kingdom
Judah (southern)—Rehoboam, son of Solomon, made king.
Israel (northern)—Jeroboam I, crowned king.

722 B.C.  Samaria falls, and many Jews carried off to Assyria. These are sometimes referred to as "The Ten Lost Tribes."

600 B.C.  Babylon gains supremacy over Assyria, and becomes the strongest power in the Orient.

586 B.C.  Jerusalem besieged and destroyed by Nebuchadnezzar and many inhabitants taken to Babylon.

538 B.C.  Cyrus, king of Persia, conquers Babylon and permits Jewish exiles to return to Jerusalem.

537 B.C.  Zerubbabel and Joshua lead the first Jews, a small group. back to Jerusalem.

516 B.C.  The Temple at Jerusalem is rebuilt. though very much less imposing than the former one.

458 B.C.  Ezra leads a second group (large) of returning exiles.

445 B.C.  Nehemiah leads third group (large) of returning exiles. Walls of Jerusalem are rebuilt.

420 B.C.  Samaritans are not accepted by the people of Jerusalem. and build their own temple on Mount Gerizim.

333 B.C.  Alexander the Great conquers Judea, and the Greek influence becomes very strong in the land.

175 B.C.  Antiochus Epiphanes becomes king of Syria, and attempts to destroy the Jewish religion.

169 B.C.  The Temple is plundered and desecrated by Antiochus Epiphanes.

167 B.C.  Mattathias kills the Syrian officer at Modin, and the Maccabean revolt begins.

165 B.C.  Judas Maccabees, son of Mattathias, drives the Romans out of Jerusalem and purifies and rededicates the Temple.

139 B.C.  Rome recognizes the Jewish state, but continual strife and unrest goes on.

 63 B.C.  Pompey of Rome captures Jerusalem.

 40 B.C.  The Parthians seize Jerusalem.

 37 B.C.  Herod with his armies recapture Jerusalem, and from Rome he is given title, "King of the Jews."

 20 B.C.  Herod rebuilds the Temple.

  6 B.C.  Jesus born in Bethlehem.

  4 B.C.  Herod dies.

 27 A.D.  Jesus crucified

 65 A.D.  Paul martyred under the emperor Nero

 70 A.D.  Titus besieges Jerusalem and destroys it. The Jews are dispersed.

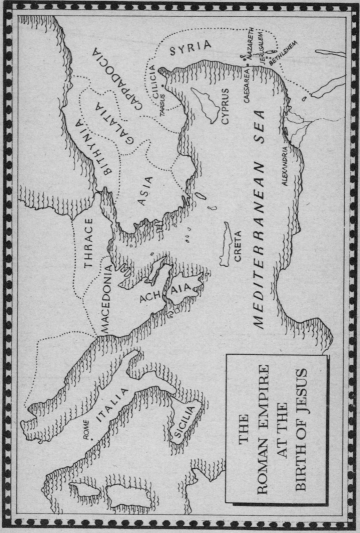

THE
ROMAN EMPIRE
AT THE
BIRTH OF JESUS

# THE ROMAN EMPIRE AT THE BIRTH OF JESUS

*Map 19*

In 63 B.C. the legions of Rome under Pompey overran Syria, and then moved on down to control the much coveted "bridge" leading to Egypt. Once more this unfortunate little land was a place of destruction, persecution and terror, to be ripped and torn by the devastating claws of the Roman eagle. The independence which they had gained under the Maccabees one hundred years earlier was now at an end. For many years ahead, the power of Rome would be dominant over the entire homeland of the Jews.

Around 40 B.C. the Parthians from a far eastern land just south of the Caspian Sea swooped down on Jerusalem and Palestine. Three years later a young man in Rome named Herod was given the title of King of the Jews, and was sent with a strong army to recapture Jerusalem and to represent the Roman Empire in that country.

The Jews disliked Herod greatly. He was a rank tyrant and showed no mercy to any one who opposed him in any way. He imposed crushing taxes upon the people to obtain the money he wanted to spend. He had a mania for building. His most spectacular achievement was the construction of a magnificent Temple for the Jews, not because of love for the God of Israel, but probably as an attempt to appease the people in their hatred of him.

When Herod realized he was about to die, he ordered that the chief men of every village in Judea should be killed when he died so that the entire country would weep at his death. Nevertheless, this last monstrous outrage was not carried out, but the imprisoned men were set free to return to their homes, and the people rejoiced at the burial of King Herod (4 B.C.).

> *About two years before the death of Herod,*
>
> *the baby Jesus was born in a stable*
>
> *in Bethlehem of Judea.*

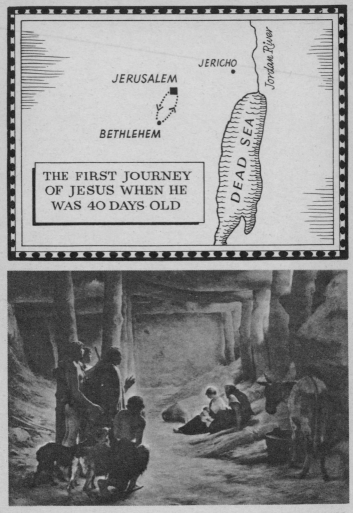

THE FIRST JOURNEY
OF JESUS WHEN HE
WAS 40 DAYS OLD

JERUSALEM

JERICHO

BETHLEHEM

Jordan River

DEAD SEA

*The Arrival of the Shepherds*     *Painting by Henri LeRolle 1848-1929*

# THE FIRST JOURNEY OF JESUS when 40 days old
## Bethlehem—Jerusalem—Bethlehem

Map 20

*Bethlehem*— The Birth of Jesus   Luke 2:1-14

Jesus was born probably 8-6 B.C. In Matthew 2 we read that Herod was still king of the province when Jesus was born, and we know Herod died in 4 B.C. The Romans made a check on the population every fourteen years, and one such count is known to have taken place in 6 A.D. While at first it may seem strange that Jesus was born before the era began that bears his name, it must be remembered that our present system of dating was not adopted until the sixth century A.D. At that time an error was made in the very complicated calculations which were involved in the attempt to work out a Christian chronology from the previous Roman system. Hence, the seeming anomaly.

— The Visit of the Shepherds   Luke 2:15-20

The shepherds were looked down upon by the orthodox religious people as they were unable to keep the details of the ceremonial law, the hand-washings and rules and regulations since they had to spend their time with their flocks. Yet it was to them that God's great message first came.

*Jerusalem*— The Presentation of Jesus in the Temple   Luke 2:22-38

On the fortieth day after Jesus' birth Mary went up to the Temple in Jerusalem, 6 miles away, to make her offering of purification, according to the Holy Law of the Jews. The offering she took consisted of a pair of turtle-doves, which the very poor were allowed to give. She carried the baby Jesus with her, and the parents marvelled at the words of Simeon and the prophetess Anna, who declared that their child was none other than the promised Messiah of Israel.

*Bethlehem*— The Visit of the Wise Men   Matthew 2:1-12

These Wise Men were probably Magi from Persia, men who were skilled in medicine and natural science, and were well-versed in astrology as well. Since the heavenly bodies represented an orderly universe, if this orderliness were broken by something unusual like the rising of a new and very bright star, it could easily suggest to the star-gazers that something exceptional was about to take place. Furthermore, just at that time there was a sense of expectancy throughout the world that new and powerful rulers were to come from Judea to rule the world. (See, Tacitus, Histories, 5:13)

35

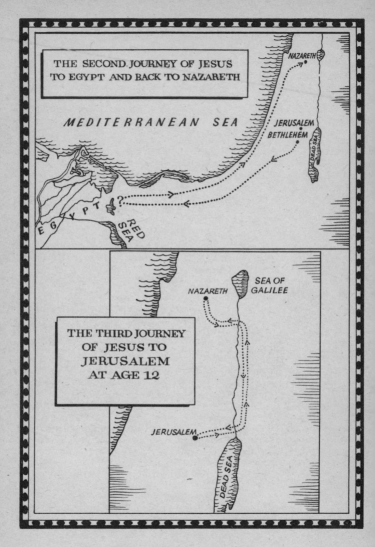

THE SECOND JOURNEY OF JESUS
TO EGYPT AND BACK TO NAZARETH

MEDITERRANEAN SEA

NAZARETH

JERUSALEM
BETHLEHEM

DEAD SEA

EGYPT

RED SEA

THE THIRD JOURNEY
OF JESUS TO
JERUSALEM
AT AGE 12

NAZARETH

SEA OF
GALILEE

JERUSALEM

DEAD SEA

## THE SECOND JOURNEY OF JESUS
### Bethlehem—Egypt—Nazareth

*Map 21*

*The Flight Into Egypt*   Matthew 2:14-23

After the departure of the Wise Men, Joseph was warned in a dream to take the child and his mother to Egypt to escape Herod's murderous intentions. There Joseph and Mary would find fellow-countrymen in every town and city, who had sought refuge in earlier years.

As to how long Mary, Joseph, and the young child stayed in Egypt, what they did there, where they lodged, we are without any clue whatever. We only know that the Scripture narrative says that when Herod died, the angel appeared again in a dream and commanded Joseph to take mother and child back into the land of Israel. So back to Nazareth, their home town, they went. The boy Jesus was probably three or four years old at the time.

## THE THIRD JOURNEY OF JESUS
### Nazareth—Jerusalem—Nazareth

*Map 22*

*The Journey to the Passover at Jerusalem*   Luke 2:41-52

The age of twelve was considered with the Jews as the time when a boy became a son of the Law and took the obligations of the Law upon himself. Therefore when his parents went to Jerusalem for the greatest of all religious festivals—the Passover. Jesus went with them this year, as he was now twelve years old.

When the caravan started homeward, Joseph and Mary missed Jesus at the first night's encampment. The women usually started out a little earlier than the men, as they travelled more slowly, and doubtless each parent thought the boy was with the other. They hurried back to Jerusalem to look for him, and there they found him in the Temple among the teachers, "listening to them and asking them questions." When Mary gently reproved her son, saying, "Behold, your father and I have been looking for you anxiously," Jesus took the word "father" and immediately applied it to his Heavenly Father: "Did you not know that I must be in my Father's house?"

Quite likely it may have been at this Passover, as he felt manhood upon him, that Jesus first felt the consciousness that in a special way, different from other men, he was the Son of God.

37

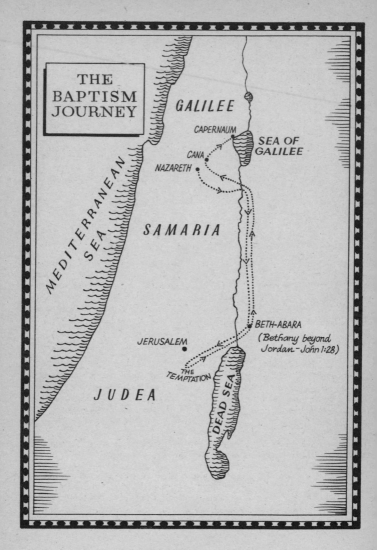

THE BAPTISM JOURNEY

GALILEE

CAPERNAUM

CANA

NAZARETH

SEA OF GALILEE

MEDITERRANEAN SEA

SAMARIA

JERUSALEM

BETH-ABARA
(Bethany beyond Jordan - John 1:28)

THE TEMPTATION

JUDEA

DEAD SEA

# THE JOURNEY FOR BAPTISM
## Nazareth—Bethabara—the Wilderness—Galilee

*Map 23*

*Nazareth*—Here Jesus lived, following that great experience in the Temple at Jerusalem, and Luke tells us that "he increased in wisdom and in stature, and in favor with God and man."

Jesus undoubtedly lived the simple life of his village. He would surely help his mother about the house, and his father in the carpenter's shop. As we hear no further mention of Joseph in the gospel records, it is assumed that he died when Jesus was still a youth. If this is so, then Jesus may have had the responsibility of caring for his mother and brothers and sisters in his father's place. But all the time we may be sure he was thinking deeply, and striving to discover the will of God His Father for him and how best to engage in it.

*Bethabara* — The Baptism  Matthew 3:13-17

Some eighteen years after the curtain of silence which hid those years in the home is lifted. Now we see the young man Jesus joining with others to go to the valley of the Jordan to see and hear John the Baptist who was preaching the coming of the Kingdom of God on earth. Wishing to identify himself with that movement, he requested that John baptize him in the Jordan.

*The Wilderness*— The Temptation  Matthew 4:1-11; Luke 4:1-13

After the baptism, Jesus went into the wilderness, probably in Judea, a desolate, barren region just west of the Dead Sea and south of Jerusalem. It was in this region that, centuries before, the prophet Amos had lived. And here, the gospel records say, Jesus stayed for forty days in meditation and prayer. And here he was tempted.

*Galilee*—After the temptation in the wilderness, Jesus went back to Bethabara, and then homeward to Galilee.

*(From now on, the Gospel narratives differ considerably, since they were written by four different men at four different times. Therefore, while our maps will indicate some of the places Jesus visited in his ministry, no attempt will be made to maintain an authentic sequence or chronology.)*

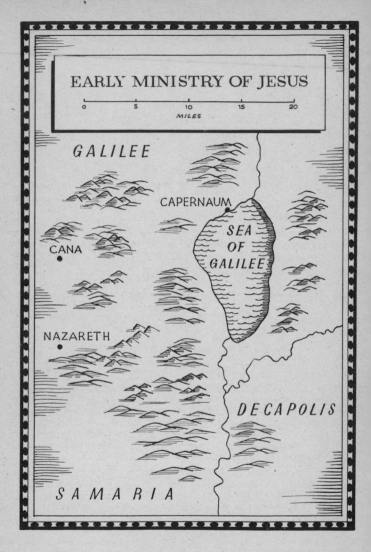

EARLY MINISTRY OF JESUS

0 5 10 15 20
MILES

GALILEE

CAPERNAUM

SEA OF GALILEE

CANA

NAZARETH

DECAPOLIS

SAMARIA

40

# THE EARLY MINISTRY OF JESUS
## in Galilee

*Map 24*

Though Jesus did not return at once to his home town of Nazareth, he did begin his public ministry in the familiar home country of Galilee. Galilee was very densely populated and the people were the least conservative of all Palestine.

*Capernaum—*

Jesus went directly to Capernaum on the northwestern shore of the Sea of Galilee. Here he began to pick a group of men who would be with him, whom he could teach, and who might carry on his work later. The first of these were fishermen whom he met at their work. Instead of seeking out the officials of organized religion, Jesus made friends with fishermen, tax collectors and others whose work did not permit them to spend much time in the synagogue or Temple, or carry out the minutiæ of religious rules as laid down by the Pharisees. Hence they were considered as irreligious and sinners. Matthew 4:18-22; John 1:43-51; Luke 6:12-16.

Some of the other events around Capernaum were:
1. The man with the unclean spirit—Mark 1:21-28
2. Healing of Peter's mother-in-law—Mark 1:29-31
3. The paralyzed man let down through the roof, and healed
    —Mark 2:1-12
4. The healing of many sick and afflicted—Matthew 4:23-25.

*Nazareth—*

Jesus taught in the synagogues and preached the gospel of the kingdom throughout all Galilee. One day he went back to Nazareth where he had been brought up and attended the synagogue on the Sabbath. Being well-known, Jesus was accepted as guest reader and was handed the book of the prophet Isaiah. He read a portion and then sat down and began to interpret what he had read. The people in the synagogue became angry and drove him out of the city. Luke 4:16-30.

*Cana—*

Jesus attended a wedding and performed his first miracle. John 2:1-11.

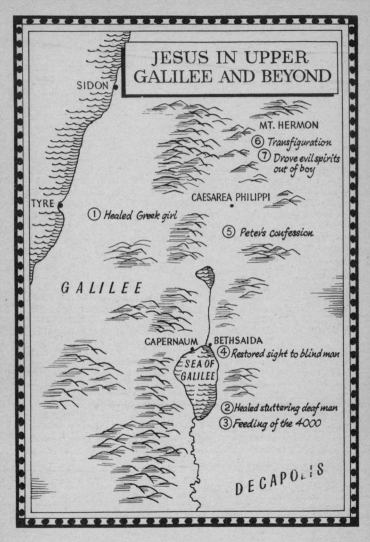

# JESUS IN UPPER GALILEE AND BEYOND

SIDON

MT. HERMON

⑥ Transfiguration
⑦ Drove evil spirits out of boy

CAESAREA PHILIPPI

TYRE

① Healed Greek girl

⑤ Peter's confession

GALILEE

CAPERNAUM   BETHSAIDA
④ Restored sight to blind man

SEA OF GALILEE

② Healed stuttering deaf man
③ Feeding of the 4000

DECAPOLIS

# JESUS IN UPPER GALILEE AND BEYOND

*Map 25*

*Region of Tyre and Sidon*  1. Healed the Greek girl.  Mark 7:24-30
   The region of Tyre and Sidon was in Phoenicia which belonged to Syria and so was outside Jewish territory.  Jesus therefore had come into the land of Gentiles.  The Scribes and Pharisees would not think of contaminating themselves by eating ceremonially unclean foods or by associating with unclean Gentiles.  Is Jesus by his action implying that the Gentiles are not unclean and may be welcomed into the kingdom of His Father?

*Region of Decapolis*  2. Healed the stuttering deaf man.  Mark 7:31-37
   The narrative says Jesus went out of the region of Tyre and went through Sidon to reach the Sea of Galilee.  A glance at the map will show that this was quite a roundabout journey.  It may have consumed eight months or so.  This would have given Jesus a long time to live closely with his disciples to teach them and prepare them before the tensions of the bitter days coming soon.

3. Fed the multitude.  Mark 8:1-10
   The gathering of a great crowd may have been due to the healing of the stuttering deaf man, and curing of the Gerasene demoniac somewhat earlier (Mark 5:1-20).

*Bethsaida*  4. Restored sight to a blind man.  Mark 8:22-26
   Blindness was a curse of that country.  It was caused by highly infectious ophthalmia, aggravated by dirt, dust and glare, and the fact that the people knew nothing of hygiene and cleanliness.

*On the Way to Caesarea Philippi*  5. Peter's confession  Mark 8:27-30.
   Here was Jesus' test to find what his disciples thought about him.  Had he succeeded in bringing them to know who he really was?

*Mount Hermon*  6. The Transfiguration.   Mark 9:2-8
   We cannot understand much of this narrative, nor do we need to.  One fact is fairly certain, however, though the disciples were confused and distraught by what Jesus had been telling them, they could only have been strongly reassured by the voice of God acknowledging Jesus as His own and charging them to listen to him.

*At the Foot of Mt. Hermon*  7. Healed the epileptic boy.  Mark 9:14-29
   On the mountain Jesus had been dealing with the great issues of the future of his work.  Now as he came down he found a very sick boy, and Jesus immediately gave himself to the boy's needs.  Nothing mattered to Jesus as much as a human need.

43

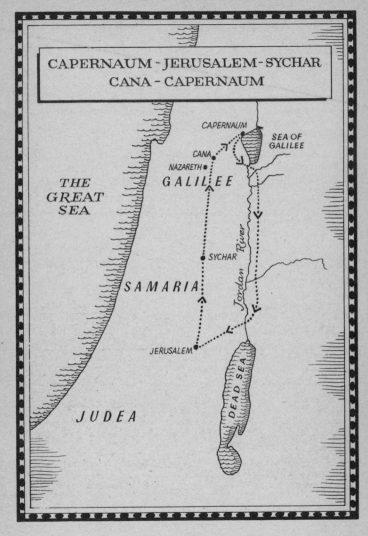

CAPERNAUM - JERUSALEM - SYCHAR
CANA - CAPERNAUM

CAPERNAUM

SEA OF
GALILEE

CANA

NAZARETH

GALILEE

THE
GREAT
SEA

Jordan River

SYCHAR

SAMARIA

JERUSALEM

DEAD SEA

JUDEA

# CAPERNAUM-JERUSALEM-SYCHAR-CANA-CAPERNAUM
## A round-trip. Capernaum to Capernaum.

*Map 26*

*1. Capernaum*

*2. Jerusalem* Jesus met Nicodemus John 3:1-21

Nicodemus was a wealthy Pharisee. He was also a member of the Sanhedrin, the supreme court of the Jews, one of whose duties was to ferret out and deal with anyone suspected of being a false prophet. It was amazing that Nicodemus went to Jesus at all. He must have been a sincere man, who felt a real lack in his life.

*3. Sychar* Jesus talked with the Woman at Jacob's Well. John 4:1-26

When Jesus left Jerusalem for Galilee he took the shortest way which led through Samaria. There was a feud of long standing between the Jews and Samaritans, and in going from Judea to Galilee or vice versa the Jews usually went down to the Jordan River, crossed over to the east side so as not to touch any of Samaria. But Jesus disregarded the foolish barrier and thereby had opportunity to talk with a Samaritan woman about the nature of God.

*4. Cana* Healed the Centurion's Son. John 4:46-53

Jesus was in Cana when this officer in Herod's court, who lived in Capernaum, came to see him. The nobleman had gone 20 miles to ask a favor of a village carpenter. Then he walked back the twenty miles with nothing but faith in Jesus' word to comfort his heart. But he was not disappointed.

*5. Capernaum*

*The Woman of Samaria*                    *William Dyce 1806-1864*

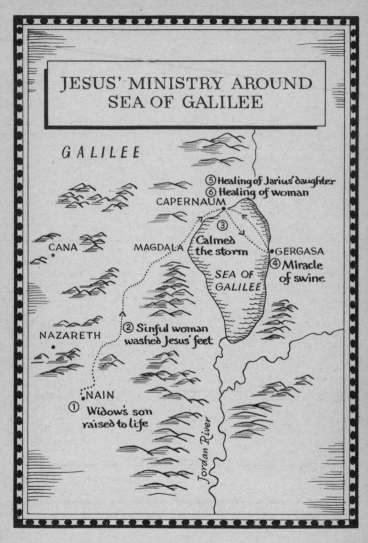

JESUS' MINISTRY AROUND
SEA OF GALILEE

GALILEE

⑤ Healing of Jarius' daughter
⑥ Healing of woman

CAPERNAUM

③

Calmed
the storm

CANA

MAGDALA

•GERGASA

④ Miracle
of swine

SEA OF
GALILEE

② Sinful woman
washed Jesus' feet

NAZARETH

① •NAIN

Widow's son
raised to life

Jordan River

46

# JESUS' MINISTRY AROUND THE SEA OF GALILEE

*Map 27*

## 1. The Widow's Son Raised to Life   Luke 7:11-17

The funeral procession would be headed by professional wailers uttering shrill cries of grief, and playing flutes and cymbals. Their purpose was to increase the sound of mourning, thus to demonstrate the great sorrow of the family and respect for the dead.

## 2. A Sinful Woman Washed Jesus' Feet   Luke 7:36-50

Somewhere in his journey taking the Good News of the Kingdom of God through Galilee, Jesus was invited to eat in the home of Simon the Pharisee. In those days guests did not sit at a table to eat, but reclined on sloping couches around three sides of a table, with the servants serving from the center. The guests rested on their left elbow, with the right arm free, and feet extended toward the end of the couch. During the meal the sandals were removed. Often a dining room was separated from the street only by a curtain. It was entirely permissible for passers-by to peer in upon the meal and listen to the conversation, especially if some rabbi were the guest. This made it easy for the woman of this incident to be at the feet of Jesus.

## 3. Jesus Calmed the Storm   Luke 8:22-25

The Sea of Galilee is prone to have sudden squalls. The surface is 600 feet below sea level. The rivers have cut deep ravines through the mountainous areas which act as tunnels to draw cold winds on to the warmer air on the water, and this causes severe tempests.

## 4. The Miracle of Swine.   Luke 8:26-33

This man who had demons was evidently a case of violent insanity. He was considered too dangerous to be at large and had been bound with chains and fetters. However, these he broke and escaped and had gone to live among the tombs, which were supposed to be the haunt of demons, and where he was less likely to be disturbed by living men.

## 5. Healed Jairus's Daughter   Luke 8:40-56

Jairus was the ruler, or president, of the synagogue, and that position was a very important one. The ruler was responsible for the administration of the Synagogue, and for the proper conduct of public worship. We may assume that the ruler was a very orthodox Jew and would have considered Jesus a dangerous heretic. Only in his desperation had he come to Jesus.

## 6. Healed the Woman with a Flow of Blood   Luke 8:43-48

The issue of blood with which this woman was afflicted made her ceremonially unclean and so cut her off from a normal life. This was why she did not come to Jesus openly, but crept up hoping to touch his garment unseen.

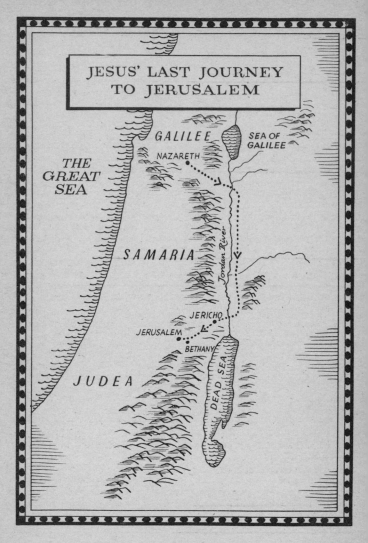

JESUS' LAST JOURNEY
TO JERUSALEM

THE GREAT SEA

GALILEE

SEA OF GALILEE

NAZARETH

SAMARIA

Jordan River

JERICHO

JERUSALEM

BETHANY

JUDEA

DEAD SEA

# JESUS' LAST JOURNEY TO JERUSALEM

*Map 28*

The time came when Jesus felt that he must leave the familiar country of Galilee and go to Jerusalem, the center of his people's life and religion. He chose the time of the Passover. Jerusalem would be crowded with people who came not only from Palestine but from the farthest reaches of the Roman Empire.

*Jericho*  Restored Sight to the Blind Man.  Luke 18:35-43

As they approached Jericho, a blind beggar insistently cried out for Jesus to restore to him his sight. Because of the man's evident faith, Jesus granted the man his request.

*Jesus and Zaccheus*  Luke 19:1-10

Jericho was a wealthy city because of her trade in dates and balsam. Therefore it was a fat taxation center. Zaccheus was a tax-collector who had reached the top of his profession, and was much hated. But Jesus saw the good in Zaccheus and made a new man of him.

*Bethany*  A Colt for the Lord  Luke 19:28-35

Bethany was less than two miles from Jerusalem at the base of the opposite side of the Mount of Olives, just before the edge of the desert hills that stretched down to Jericho. Bethphage is unknown today but was evidently a small settlement near Bethany.

*Jerusalem*  The Triumphal Entry  Luke 19:36-40

This entry into Jerusalem was sheer courage on the part of Jesus. He deliberately planned to enter the city in such a way as to focus attention on himself and to dramatize the claim that he was the Messiah, God's anointed king (Zachariah 9:9). He did this knowing that orders had been given out to arrest him on sight, that a price was on his head.

*The Cleansing of the Temple*  Matthew 21:12,13.  Luke 19:45,46

Every male Jew paid a Temple tax every year, and it had to be paid in Jewish currency, even though the man came from another country. The money changers made an unreasonable charge for this service. Animals without blemish had to be brought for sacrifice and must pass the inspectors. It was safer to purchase these at booths in the Temple, even though they were priced outrageously high for the gain of the priests. Thus were the people imposed on inside the Temple.

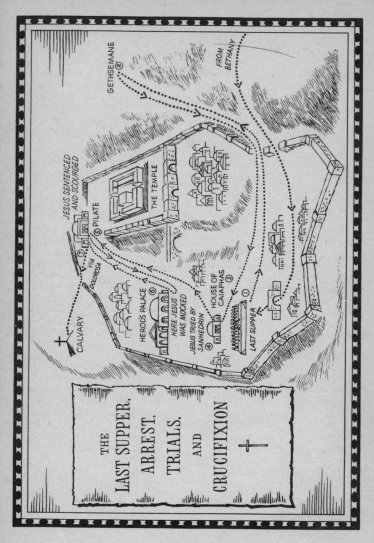

THE
LAST SUPPER,
ARREST,
TRIALS,
AND
CRUCIFIXION

GETHSEMANE ②

FROM BETHANY

THE TEMPLE

JESUS SENTENCED AND SCOURGED

PILATE ⑤

VIA DOLOROSA ⑦

CALVARY

HEROD'S PALACE ⑥

HERE JESUS WAS MOCKED

JESUS TRIED BY SANHEDRIN ④

HOUSE OF CAIAPHAS ③

LAST SUPPER ①

# THE LAST SUPPER. ARREST. TRIALS. and CRUCIFIXION
Map 29 in and around Jerusalem

## 1. The Last Meal Together   Luke 22:7-23

Most houses of that day looked like a box with a smaller box on top. The small box on top was the upper room, reached by a stairway on the outside. Here it was that Jesus met with his disciples and it was this meal that he commended his disciples to repeat in remembrance of him. Today we call this observance the "Sacrament of the Lord's Supper." A Sacrament is something which has gained a meaning far beyond the thing itself, for the one who understands that meaning.

## 2. The Garden of Gethsemane   Luke 22:39-53

After the supper, Jesus and his disciples went to a garden on the side of the Mount of Olives. Wealthy persons owned private gardens there and it may be that some friend had given Jesus the privilege of using his, to which the Master might retire and relax when he felt the need. Judas would know Jesus' habit of going to this secluded spot and it was to here that he led officials from the Temple that they might take him into custody.

## 3. Jesus Before Caiaphas the High Priest
### Matthew 26:57-75; Luke 22:54-62

This was merely an unofficial examination. Afterward Jesus was put in the hands of the Temple police for safekeeping until morning, since the Sanhedrin could not meet during hours of darkness.

## 4. Jesus Before the Sanhedrin   Luke 22:66-71

The Sanhedrin was composed of seventy members representing Scribes, Pharisees, Rabbis, Priests, Sadducees and Elders. This body was the supreme court of the Jews in religion and theology, and it was only in this field that they talked with Jesus. They had no authority to pronounce or carry out the death sentence.

## 5. Jesus Before Pilate   Luke 23:1-6

Since the Jews could not carry out a death sentence, they sent Jesus to the Roman governor, Pilate. By subtly hinting at political and seditious agitation, they hoped Pilate would take drastic action with Jesus. Pilate saw through their scheming, however. When he learned that Jesus was a Galilean and therefore belonged in Herod's jurisdiction, he was relieved to send Jesus to Herod, who happened to be in Jerusalem at the time.

## 6. Jesus Before Herod   Luke 23:7-12

Herod treated Jesus as of no importance.—laughed at him. mocked him. and then sent him back to Pilate.

## 7. Jesus Again Before Pilate   Luke 23:13-25; John 18:28-19:16

Pilate fell back on the custom of releasing a prisoner selected by the will of the people at the Passover Feast. Their verdict was that Barabbas. a thief. should be released. and Jesus be put to death. and to please the people Pilate ordered this.

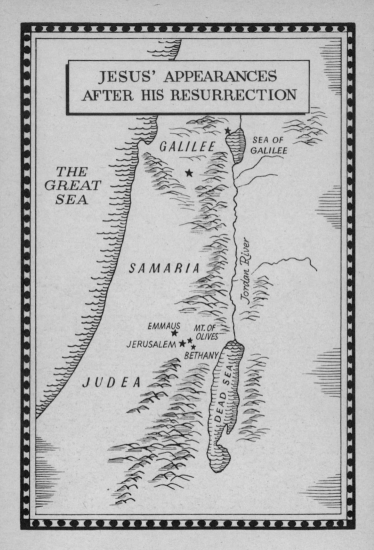

JESUS' APPEARANCES
AFTER HIS RESURRECTION

GALILEE

SEA OF
GALILEE

THE
GREAT
SEA

SAMARIA

Jordan River

EMMAUS
MT. OF
OLIVES
JERUSALEM
BETHANY

JUDEA

DEAD SEA

# JESUS' APPEARANCES AFTER HIS RESURRECTION

*Map 30*

*Jerusalem*
    To Mary outside the tomb                      John 20:11-18
    To the two Marys                              Matthew 28:1-10
    To disciples, Thomas absent                   John 20:19-23
    To disciples, Thomas present                  John 20:26-29

*Emmaus*
    To two disciples                              Luke 24:13-35

*Galilee*
    To disciples by the sea                       John 21
    To disciples on the mountain                  Matthew 28:16-20

*Mount of Olives*
    To the disciples, at his ascension            Luke 24:50-53
                                                  Acts 1:1-11

*The Supper at Emmaus    Painting by Leon A. L'Hermitte 1844-1925*

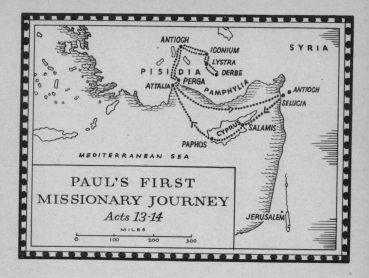

PAUL'S FIRST
MISSIONARY JOURNEY
Acts 13-14

MILES
0    100    200    300

### SAUL—later called Paul

To carry out the mission which Jesus gave them, his followers created a fellowship which was known as the church. Many converts were made. The Jewish authorities were against this new movement and some of the followers were persecuted, stoned, and imprisoned. (Acts 1-7)

One of the most aggressive of these persecutors was a young man named Saul. On one occasion Saul set out for Damascus with authority to find there any who were of the Jesus Way and bring them bound to Jerusalem. On the road, he had a startling vision in which Jesus appeared and spoke to him. As a result, Saul himself became an active follower of Jesus, whom he now called the Christ, the Son of God. (Acts 8—9:22)

At first the followers were afraid of him, for they remembered how he had arrested and imprisoned many of their number. But one man, Barnabas, brought Saul to the apostles and told them of Saul's experiences and the great change that had taken place. Some years later Barnabas and Saul became a part of the church in Syrian Antioch. (Acts 9:23—12:25)

54

(1100 miles)
Acts 13 and 14

*Map 31*

*Ant´ioch in Syria*—The followers of Christ were first called Christians
    in Antioch. This church sent Saul, Barnabas and John
    Mark on a preaching tour.

*Seleu´cia*—Here they embarked for Cyprus.

*Sal´amis*—Preached in the synagogue.

*Paph´os*—El´ymas made blind.
    From now on, Saul was called Paul.

*Per´ga*—John Mark left Paul and Barnabas and returned to Jeru-
    salem.

*Antioch in Pisidia*—Paul preached in the synagogue and the people
    wanted more the next Sabbath.
        Jealous Jews contradicted and reviled Paul and
    Barnabas.
            Paul told them he would now turn to the Gentiles.
        The Jews stirred up trouble and persecution and
    drove Paul and Barnabas out of the city.

*Īcōn´ium*—Paul and Barnabas spoke in the synagogue, but were stoned.

*Lystra*—Paul healed a cripple.
        Jews from Antioch and Iconium nearly stoned Paul
    to death and dragged him outside the city.

*Der´be*—Paul and Barnabas preached here for a time and made
    disciples.

*Lystra, Iconium and Antioch*—Paul and Barnabas retraced their
    steps, strengthened and exhorted the recent converts.

*Per´ga*—Preached here.

*Attalī´a* — Embarked for Antioch in Syria

*Antioch*—Gathered the church together and told of their experiences,
    and how God had opened the door of faith to the Gen-
    tiles, also.

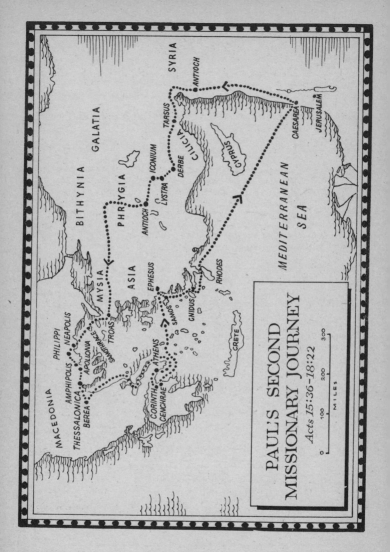

PAUL'S SECOND
MISSIONARY JOURNEY
*Acts 15:36–18:22*

MILES
0    100    200    300

# PAUL'S SECOND MISSIONARY JOURNEY
## (2500 miles)
### Acts 15:36-18:22

*Map 32*

*Antioch in Syria*—Paul and Silas start out together to visit the churches where Paul had previously preached.

*Tar′sus*—Paul's home city.

*Derbe, Lystra, Icōn′ium, Antioch* — Here they were joined by Timothy, a young Christian.

*Tro′as*—Vision of man beseeching.—"Come over into Macedonia and help us."
> Acts 16:10    From now on, the narrative continues in the first person plural, "we"—showing that the account is being told by someone in the party with Paul, probably Luke the Physician. It is possible that Paul's health was not good and Luke went along to keep him in as good condition as possible. This ailment, or ill health, may have been the thorn in the flesh to which Paul made reference in II Corinthians 12:7.

*Sam′othrace Neap′olis*

*Philippi*—Lydia baptized.
> Paul and Silas arrested and put in prison.
> Baptism of the jailer and his whole family.

*Amphip′olis, Appolon′ia*

*Thessaloni′ca*—Here Paul proclaimed Christ for three weeks, despite disturbances.

*Berē′a*—Many converts, but the people were stirred up by Jews who came on from Thessalonica.
> Silas and Timothy remained here while Paul went on to Athens.

*Athens*—Paul came here by sea. Argued with Epicurean and Stoic philosophers. Preached from the Areop′a gus.

*Corinth*—Preached in the synagogue every Sabbath. Silas and Timothy rejoined Paul. Much opposition, but they remained in Corinth a year and a half.

*Eph′esus*— Paul preached in the synagogue.
> Set sail for Syria.

*Caesarea*—Paul landed here, greeted the church, and went back to Antioch.

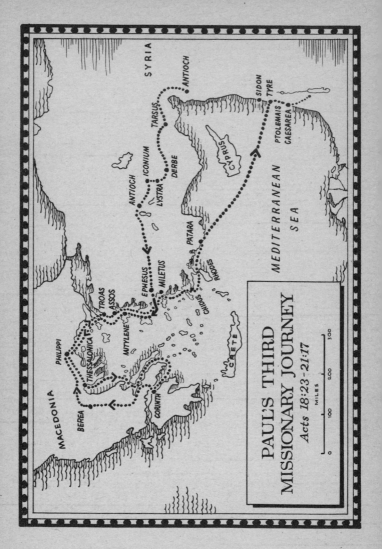

SYRIA

ANTIOCH

TARSUS

SIDON
TYRE

PTOLEMAIS
CAESAREA

ANTIOCH

ICONIUM

LYSTRA

DERBE

CYPRUS

MEDITERRANEAN

SEA

PATARA

RHODES

EPHESUS

MILETUS

CNIDUS

TROAS

ASSOS

MITYLENE

CRETE

PHILIPPI

THESSALONICA

MACEDONIA

BEREA

CORINTH

## PAUL'S THIRD
## MISSIONARY JOURNEY
### Acts 18:23 - 21:17

MILES

0    100    200    300

# PAUL'S THIRD MISSIONARY JOURNEY
## (2800 miles)
### Acts 18:23—21:17

*Map 33*

*Antioch in Syria*—Departed from Antioch.

*Derbe, Lystra, Iconium, Antioch*—Revisited these churches.

*Eph′esus*—Paul baptized, and proclaimed the kingdom of God. Stayed over two years.
> Opposed by a wealthy maker of silver shrines because Paul preached that gods made by hand were not real gods.

*Macedōn′ia*—Paul sailed for Macedonia, encouraged the churches there, and went on to Greece.

*Greece*—Stayed for three months then started homeward, once more going through Macedonia.

*Philippi*—Stayed here for a few days, then sailed for Troas.

*Troas*—The night before Paul was to leave Troas he spoke to people in an upper room. While he was talking, a young man sitting in the window went to sleep and fell three stories.

*Milē′tus*—At Miletus Paul sent to Ephesus and had the elders of the church there come down to see him. He told them that he was going back to Jerusalem and might face persecution and imprisonment there. He added that he probably would not see them again and commended them to God and urged them to be faithful to Him.

*Pat′ara*—Here they were able to find a ship crossing to Phoenicia, so they went aboard and sailed to Tyre.

*Tyre*—Paul and his party sought out the Christian followers here, and remained with them for seven days.

*Ptolemā′is*—Greeted the Christian brethren here and remained for a day.

*Caesarea*—Remained here with Philip the evangelist. While here, it was dramatically predicted that Paul would definitely be imprisoned if he went to Jerusalem.
> "I am ready not only to be imprisoned but even to die at Jerusalem for the name of the Lord Jesus."

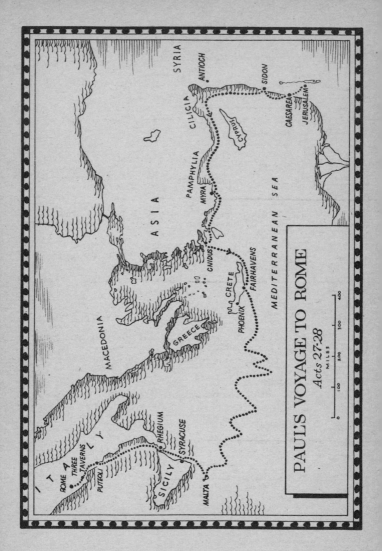

PAUL'S VOYAGE TO ROME

*Acts 27-28*

MILES

0   100   200   300   400

MEDITERRANEAN SEA

SYRIA
ANTIOCH
SIDON
CILICIA
CYPRUS
CAESAREA
JERUSALEM
PAMPHYLIA
MYRA
ASIA
CNIDUS
CRETE
FAIRHAVENS
PHOENIX
MACEDONIA
GREECE
ITALY
ROME
THREE TAVERNS
PUTEOLI
RHEGIUM
SYRACUSE
SICILY
MALTA

# PAUL'S VOYAGE TO ROME
## (1800 miles)
## Acts 27. 28

Map 34

*Caesarea*—Paul and some other prisoners in charge of a Roman centurion set sail. probably from Caesarea.

*Sidon*—The ship stopped here and Paul was allowed a brief visit with friends.

*Myra*—Apparently this was the terminal for the ship in which they had embarked.
   The centurion found another ship about to sail for Italy. so put his prisoners aboard it.

*Fair Havens. Island of Crete*—Paul warned that the voyage would end in disaster. but the captain of the ship decided to set sail.

*Malta*—As the result of a terrific northeast storm. the ship was beached on the island called Malta.
   After three months they secured passage in another ship and continued on their way.

*Syracuse. Island of Sicily*—The ship put in here for three days.

*Rhegium*—This was the first port at which they touched the mainland of Italy itself.
   They remained here only one day. until a favorable wind came up.

*Puteō′li*—Paul met here some of the Christian brethren and even though he was a prisoner he was permitted to stay with them for seven days.

*Rome*—Rome at last! and Paul was allowed to have his own living quarters. with only a soldier to guard him.
   Here Paul continued to live for two years. and taught and preached Jesus Christ openly and unhindered. From here he sent letters to individuals and Christian congregations throughout the Roman world.
   It is thought that Paul was put to death during the reign of the infamous emperor. Nero.

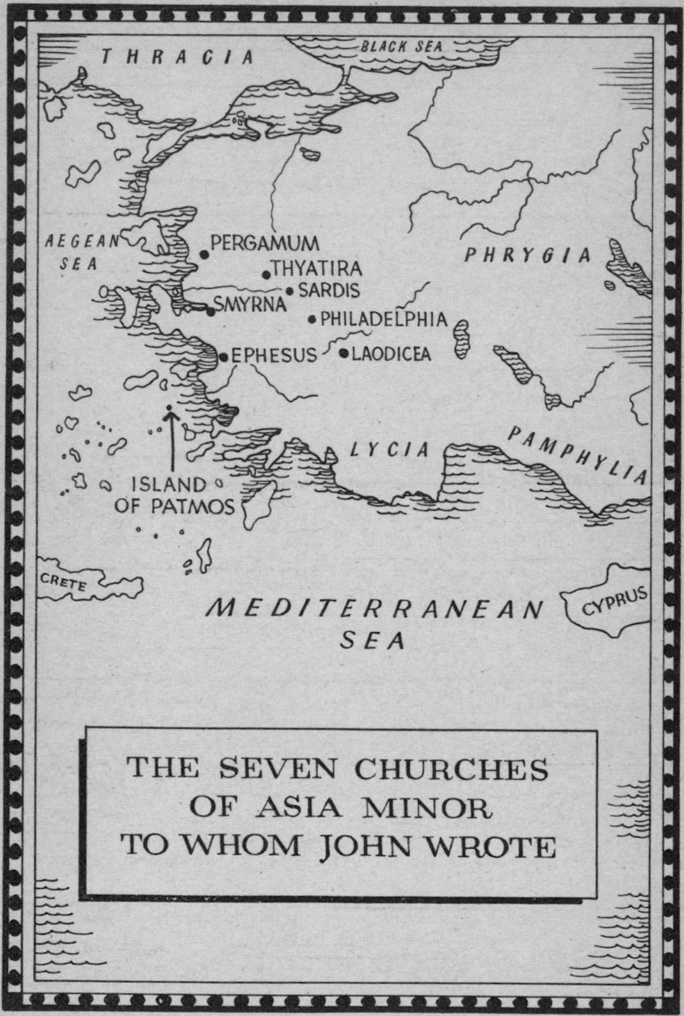

THRACIA

BLACK SEA

AEGEAN SEA

PERGAMUM

THYATIRA

SMYRNA • SARDIS

PHILADELPHIA

EPHESUS • LAODICEA

PHRYGIA

ISLAND OF PATMOS

LYCIA

PAMPHYLIA

CRETE

MEDITERRANEAN SEA

CYPRUS

## THE SEVEN CHURCHES OF ASIA MINOR TO WHOM JOHN WROTE

# THE SEVEN CHURCHES IN ASIA
The Revelation to John, Chapters 1, 2, and 3.

*Map 35*

The last book in the Bible was written by a man named John. It is quite certain that he was not John the Apostle, but was evidently a Christian and one who had been persecuted for his faith, even as those to whom he was writing. He was probably banished to the island of Patmos by the Roman Emperor because of his Christian testimony. Patmos is forty miles off the coast of Asia Minor, and is ten miles long and five miles wide.

John states that he is writing letters to seven churches which are in Asia, and that would naturally mean that part of Asia which is in the Roman province. He gives the names of the seven churches as: Ephesus, Smyrna, Pergamum, Thyatira, Sardis, Philadelphia, and Laodicea. A look at the map will show that these seven cities are set down in two lines,—north and south—one line of three cities near the coast and the other of four cities crossing through the interior. The cities are about the same distance apart and cover fairly well this central part of the province. A letter sent to anyone of these seven cities could easily be circulated to other churches in the immediate area, and thus seven letters would reach a greater number of people than just those within the seven cities.

The fact that John writes to seven churches has brought an interesting thought from some commentators. The people of that day were much influenced by numerology. The number *seven* was considered as the perfect number by ancient peoples. Seven stands for completeness. Seven is the combination of four and three. Three is the divine number, symbol of the Trinity. Four is the cosmic number, since to primitive man the earth was flat with four boundaries and four corners. So when the divine and the cosmic are added to make seven, the result is the symbol of perfection, the heavenly plus the earthly—completeness.

John's letters were to seven churches, but the number seven suggests that what he writes is for the *entire church*, everywhere, even down the centuries to today.

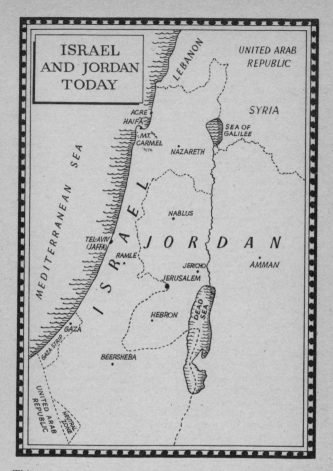

ISRAEL AND JORDAN TODAY

This map shows the entire Palestine of Jesus' day which was partitioned into Jewish (Israel) and Arab (Jordan) states by the United Nations in 1947. Independence was proclaimed by the State of Israel on May 14, 1948, the day the British mandate ended.